The Sinew of Forty Seven Years

poems by

Sarah Sandman

Finishing Line Press
Georgetown, Kentucky

The Sinew of Forty-Seven Years

ACKNOWLEDGMENTS

Thank you to all the readers of my work who have helped these poems come to
life. I appreciate you all.
Thank you to my circle of women who support me as I walk this path.
Thank you to my writing mentors near and far.

Publisher: Leah Maines

Editor: Christen Kincaid

Cover Art: Rachel Hartley-Smith

Author Photo: Sarah Sandman

Cover Design: Elizabeth Maines

Printed in the USA on acid-free paper.
Order online: www.finishinglinepress.com
            also available on amazon.com

Author inquiries and mail orders:
Finishing Line Press
P. O. Box 1626
Georgetown, Kentucky 40324
U. S. A.

Table of Contents

for the wise woman who sits across from me each week,
for Kate and Skylar,
and for Dori, always

Filled with Salt and Water
—to my soldier

I want. I wish.
These stories—
I wish you were here
in corporeal form, embodied
from my imagination, filled with salt and water,
able to touch fingertip to fingertip
gently pressing your life into me.

Our war stories are different.

I won't let my students
misuse the word "hard," but these stories
that drift from your clenched jaw
make me want to hold
your knee while looking
to your blue eye,
saying: *I am here. I witness you.*

I wish you were here, with me now,
with me here, now, with me,
touching ripped cuticles,
our nerves both on high alert.

Your beard stubble is one
of my favorite human artifacts.

I may never understand how you can witness me,
quietly re-telling you of the first times—
the first times I learned rape.
Your only hesitation
is the right-eye-lid twitch
and the hitch of your breath.

It's hard to learn rape and death.

Your man-hands have never hurt me,
but they have held
a gun, a grenade, a handful
of oppressed-Iraqi-sand.
They've held my words—
the tip of the dull desert razor
will never replace the absence
of your facial hair next to my cheek.

For us, rape and death   are.

Dying Father

"Unholy battered old thing you were, my sunflower O
my soul, I loved you then!"
—Allen Ginsberg, "Sunflower Sutra"

Prophecy is old thread,
beaten up,
italicized in the *Times,*
spun on Fox
until all you hear is dooms-
day 2012. You wish
this world, this haze,
this twitter-friend-text me mafia
would die off,
would turn dream-like,
would rest by your quiet angst.

Prophecy is tomato soup can
and vulgar stream of consciousness.

Prophecy is mime and copy and
mimic and doomsday keeps
coming back in my head—
when all I want is a sunflower,
painted or real,
taller than not.

Don't you see you're dying each time
you don't know what I say—
each time you vomit from the past?

The Cold War happened, okay?
Don't you see—I don't get to
prophesy anymore—you did it.
McCarthy and pinko, just a little
red—what's left for me?

I want to write all night,
but the paper is running low,
the pen is out of ink. My eyes
blur with repressed memories
of Japan, Korea, Afghanistan,
Iraq, Iran, I can't
go on.

My best friend drowns in medical bills,
a sick gall bladder, removed—the thought
of her death—fuck it all—take the apocalypse,
because her death would smother
my keep-living-will.
The bills—stacked—too much to pay
because she can't afford.

You can only eat macaroni for so long.

For undeliverable mail only.

Over and over, all I can hear and see
is Allen and Rockland—union
of wandering souls wrapped
in billowing cigarette smoke,
wishing for
hash or pot or hash or pot—
can't you see, I'm dying here?

But no, just wait. Just wrong.
I won't give in to the beatings, rapes,
torture, poverty, hunger. I won't give up
to the [whatever-you-want] [insert here].

This isn't a time for bending over, sucking out,
blowing in; this isn't a time for kissing feet
and thinking ass—this is a time
for Holy   unadulterated   spirituality.
Pray to your God, my God, my tree, my pen, my sun.
And yes, my friend, the sun rising
is God.

I Want My Knees

I lay with my sternum facing the ceiling, and my arms wide open. I haven't laid this open in maybe forever. I let my arms dangle, noticing the pillow under my back. The unnatural arch forces my chest to break free from the safety I normally hold it in. And so, I lay here with my sternum facing the ceiling. I take a few breaths—amazed at how wonderfully simple air is, amazed at the inflowing of the divine that rushes to my heart center. I take a few more breaths and pull my knees upward, placing my feet flat on the cushioned table. She says, do you want your knees like that? I instinctively try to put them back down. I wonder what the problem is. She says, *I know this is a vulnerable position.* I want my knees. I *want* my knees.

She says, I know you want your knees—it's about protection— you're safe here. I put my knees down and ever so gently she takes my right arm and stretches it, massaging the trigger points, grazing my fingers with hers. I wonder how she can be so gentle with my pain, so wise with my seeping emotions. I keep my focus on each of her fingers—reminding myself, *this is now.* Eventually, I feel the urge, the internal shake that always begins in the largest muscle of my leg, twitch, twitch, like the silent second hand pacing from the clock near my head. Eventually, I feel her hands, placed strategically over that large muscle, waiting, waiting. I try to remember to breathe. When she finishes, she says, you've made so much progress—you've come so far. I can still feel the twitching— still hoping I won't turn into a convulsion. I say, but my legs, and the shaking. Her eyes understand something about my soul. But my legs. But the shaking.

She says, don't worry, don't worry, *I'll wait.*

Remembering the Sandy Hook School Shooting, December 14, 2012

—for the little girl

I wish I knew your name
because you were not listed
in the headlines,
but if I did,
it would all be too real,
too horrible   a nightmare
of your truth
and my dissociated memories.

I know that you are six
and all of your classmates
are gone now   dead.

> *Mommy I'm okay.*

I know that you pretended.
Draped yourself
on a pile of other children,
playing possum,
      with the crazy   motherfucker
         who lost his mind.
      I can't think of you very often.

      I remember
you pretended to be dead.

Six years old—the only survivor in your classroom,
escaping the building when the angry shooter was gone.

My therapist, graying with wisdom,
tells me:
that girl,
      that six year old girl,
        the one who survived,
bloody, but alive,
she reminds me
      of you.

Mommy, I'm okay.

The Space Before His Hair Begins

His feet kick the Speed Racer sheets,
and I'm reminded, now the aunt and much older,
of my own six-year-old feet,
but his, free from the baggage
of incest and abuse. He doesn't care
about dying—I turn up Carole King.
His innocence and curly-hair,
fuzzy from my fingers
tugging on the tight ringlets,
makes my breath catch. He licks his lip
until a ring of red surrounds. He sleeps,
snoring gently, sweating from the heat of winter,
never waking in fear. Sometimes I wonder
how he can be so safe. Each time I kiss the space
before his hair begins and his forehead ends, each time
he says, "I just love you so much," each time
he comes home untouched   I am lucky.

In my Bones

I feel the pit of my stomach
caving in on itself, but not from hunger,
not from malnutrition,
from a sadness so deep
I can only attempt
to approximate its existence.
I think of an eight-year-old
version of myself, afraid
to breathe, to move,
afraid to live.
Her life, filled with a war-torn
home. A war of incest, of abuse,
of oppression. Her life
just an approximation of existence.
I fall to my knees—
I yearn for the words to explain,
but I'm left with none.
I can't—I can't.
This sadness, this in-my-bones-fear,
this   I can't.

I Heard the Rape Come Right out of My Mouth

I heard the Canada come right out of his mouth. It trickled off his lip—Vancouver, and the work holiday. It made me stop eating the Miso soup. I held my breath stopping the scallion from moving. Then I wondered what really comes out of my mouth—flowing like wet cement, dancing like British Columbia. I think about my memory hangover—similar to too much red wine, and yet. The pain between my leg and my leg slams like a dehydrated headache. I think about the rape that comes right out of my mouth. Shuddering and hiding my face. I don't want to remember any more if it means *this* pain. I don't want to remember any more if it means brick. I heard the rape come right out of my mouth when I tried to say Canada.

The Sinew of 900 Years

An otter holds hands with her mate to keep tethered to the one who helps fight the loam. Salt and whiskers dripping in late night tumult. I can't escape the salt of this raven call—incessant chatter since 4 a.m. What possibly is left to say? She writes me seven letters. Each in a different colored envelope. Their words are profoundly hand written and I trace the commas. She said I fill the space she's been saving—but for what, she did not know. The guarded hollow meant for something sacred, dandelion-esque. A sheltered Kodachrome. But I am no such thing. I hold all the life of blood and flesh and sweat. She's carved out that place for me from the sinew of 900 years, carved out before she knew bone was salt, before she knew *to carve* meant *to write in the sky with a toe nail.* Before she knew that *to care* was a phrase learned only on the back of a closed eye lid.

Just Never

This is not a love letter. This doesn't end with me touching your
    small breasts,
or looking into your hazel-shifting-green, depending-on-the-day-
    hazel eye.
This doesn't end with me holding you close
while I hear the rise of your sleeping rib.

This just isn't a love poem, not what you think, or thought.
This is anti-love. This is about all that there wasn't
in the space too big to fill.

I was only ever perfect, never—
you see. Just never.

Once I wrote a Surrealist Peruvian ode—just for you,
and I wanted to slurp you like vegetarian soba noodles only pausing
    for—
no, not ever pausing. I meant it then—but you—I was just never.
Never.   Love is too abstract.
They'll tell me it's been too long for this now, and I'll say no,
it's been just long enough. They'll say just pick around the chicken,
and let go. And I'll say this isn't chicken anymore.

You always knew the line, the green and the hazel,
that was for you, my past love, gone—and maybe never had.

I don't eat meat anymore,
the rotting flesh hurting my broken back—
my lame excuse for humanity.

And this is not about love—
it's about the mold inside the uncut avocado

and it's about unfilled bellies,
and dead children murdered for insanity;
it's about a black crow,
and a snowy white owl,
about the prayer beads that have always been mine.

It's about you kissing the space between my hairline and eyebrow,
whispering: *you are safe.*

My tattooed foot says believe—
I was only ever perfect, never.

dear M.

Dear Rhinoceros, my brown beautiful,

Maybe I will write a letter in reverse to you, my new love, a woman draped in a gentle tear with a face turned toward hope—my love, dear, I am the color of your nail bed. I will always be whiter than your foot, whiter than the tree-lined-circle of your iris. I come from decadent parties and accessories meant to cover and dazzle. Like a drooping dandelion, broken harp string. No, an ostrich in the sand. Hide. Hide. Dear my love, I am—hide. We curl near on the fuchsia-sheeted mattress. My eyes turn little and I disappear into the count. I stoically stroke your raised goose bump. You cannot contain anymore. I tell you, dear rhinoceros, I survived. I touch your chocolate horn. And then you weep like I've never witnessed before. You weep. He still lives by the artificial machine that prompts his heart to beat. I curl closer to you—holding tight the soft underside of your naked arm.

I have accepted this life.

The Benefit of Doubt

Perhaps fibromyalgia, unexplainable body pain—a visit to the quick clinic, no infection found, just a muse of a grief-stricken bladder. Body workers perplexed by persistent inflammation. 5 bulging discs, overly tight hips, shoulders that unhinge when upside down. An inability to cry, usually. Night terrors. A partner who gently holds face after hearing memory. No visible scars from father. Four foot tattoos. 300 nights per year, for at least 20 years. If I give him the benefit of the doubt.

You want to hold my hand

You stand sideways, chest concave. Worn down from time and the weight of our secrets. Stained by what was and could have been. Your hand always wringing. I remember every crease, fingerprint, manicured nail. You want to hold my hand and I stare in the eyes that have watched and watched. I sit in a dimly lit room, father, because the memory keeper is awake. I try to comfort her wandering feet, but she sees your ghost. Your death will be my blessing.

"You ain't never known death 'till you seen it.
You ain't never known evil 'till you lived it."

You May Think I Would Be Happy With This News

I hoped the Chinese Restaurant
would womb me
from talk of the previous life—
maybe the Crab Rangoon could divert
us to a different time,
not my birthday,
not my mother.

This story has never been about food.

And still, slipped in, a side whisper,
a glance, he *only* weighs 154 pounds.
It only takes that much—don't you understand.
It only takes that much
and then not even the sleeping pup paws,
the calm in and out breath of the wet nose,
none of that. It only takes
one moment to pull me.

It's my birthday
and my monster-father
is disintegrating.

Shaking Hands at Noon

It's like placating a fool,
to tell me
everything will be okay—
that the nightmares will stop.
Someday the flashbacks,
and the tremors,
and my shaking hands at noon,
and someday.

But today is not that someday—
today is filled with just one flash,
one thought,
not of the stacked laundry,
underwear thrown in a corner,
not of the smell of trash,
dog vomit on the rug—
not these things.

It's like placating a child
telling her that someday
she won't need.

Today, a reminder that you
rewired my DNA.
The one thought:
I want you inside me—
to feel you one last time
before you die,
to know you love me.

This thought
to feel you one last time,
the dog vomit on the rug,
the smell of trash
and shame—
the snot running down my face.

Because today is not that someday.

Dear Benevolent Dictator—

You came to me as if in a dream. Out of the corner of my eye, I could see you walking toward me from my pocket full of Hell. I was a trained-child-rape-victim. I knew what to expect. And so, slyly, you moved toward me as if I wouldn't see the wolf in your eye, as if I wouldn't smell the death in your mouth. You came to eat me— you came to take all that I had to offer. I want to say I acquiesced gracefully—I want to say I conceded. I want to say this because you, *fucker*, you *god damn* Castro, you took away my—. I turned my head away from your venom, holding my breath. I turned my head away from your Ho Chi Minh, your Lenin. I hid in my mental darkness because of you, Benevolent Dictator.

No Him, No He

You are dying in my mind,
slowly losing strength
in the large-veined hand that once
touched my face.
You are dying—
and there is no other pronoun,
no him, no he. Just you.
I cannot not write this to you—
right now, twisting in my gut,
guilt rises instead of bile.
I am dripping in my private shame.

You want me to come home
to feed you ham
and tomatoes. Right now
I cannot not write this to you.
I cannot make you the sandwich
with spicy deli mustard
that would add weight
to your emaciated form.
I cannot say no
                                    say yes
say no to you.

If Salt Were Turquoise

I.
She painted, and I wrote poems. Sometimes I grabbed her paint brush. I'd paint her body until all the parts she hated were covered up. Her lips touched mine. My string of semicolons wrapped her spliced comma. The turquoise paint smudged my leg, smudged my eye. Come back to me just this once.

II.

If salt were turquoise,
I'd mix it with rhododendron petals
and sprinkle them on your gallbladder void,
whispering alphabetic numbers—
kissing your tender flesh
with my wearied lips.

Snow moss and Virginia worm fences
cover the fields where battle
killed the husbands
and sons. She told us
about 1961, no blacks allowed.
A hawk flies low.
What would I do
without you,   no
blacks allowed. No,
            not without you.

Sky Baby

—for Skylar Catherine, April 24th, 2014

Dear Sky Baby,
today I watched you come
into this big, bright world.
Your mother and father glowing
with new-parent love,
gram and pops gently holding you
for the first time. You belong here,
little one, to this family, to *your* family.

I watched as your hair peaked
out of the canal, just one more push.
I watched as your face emerged
and there you were—all of you,
in that doctor's hands. All the fingers,
and toes. I kept your mother's grip,
watched as the world around me
ceased to exist. There was no one—
just you—for just then. And my heart chakra
spilled amber light.

You, little sky baby, will never understand
how your first breath
was like mine too—how your birth
opened a space in me. A space
named *hope*.

Cry Me Aunt

Since my friend's belly
was big enough to protrude
like a pouting lip,
I couldn't keep my hands
away. She let me touch
the magic of a life forming—
the most instinctual act
we know. I felt the energy
rise and fall, my hands warming,
connecting, my smile sneaking.

And then four days later,
four days old, no more belly,
just baby who fits in the palm
of my too-large hand.
I cradle her head,
her blue eyes open. She is not my baby,
but I will love her still.
I will hold her tiny,
and kiss her newborn cheek. She is not
my baby, but I will watch
her grow. I will remember
our magic. I will put her near my sternum,
and maybe she will cry me aunt,
while her momma stumbles
into desperate postpartum sleep.

She is not my baby,
but I will love her still.

This Thing of Gentle Opening

I don't know how to do this—
this *thing*
of gentle opening.
I have only ever known
how to be ripped apart,
forced, raped.
But this thing, so *tender*.

I don't want the past
to follow me. I don't want to curl up—
I want to pretend
that I was not visited by my father's
desire for twenty seven years.

I sit across from your beautiful brown
as the sun quenches your need
for just a little more Vitamin D,
and my mind is paused—
that beautiful brown is like nothing
I have touched. I want to trace
the curves of the golden, and milky.

But here I am, all of me.
There is no hiding anymore—
there is no denying what these eyes
have recorded for so long.

I wish I could tell you
that when he dies,
when the oxygen stops,
when his heart fails,
when there is no more monster,
I will be free. But
here I am,
all of me.
Not rounded and smooth,
just jagged.

And Forty Seven Years

I knew in the eye blink
of sitting across the speckled table
that I would fall head
over face
over ankle bone—
fall for the slightly bent
neck leaning toward the peeking sun—
mouth filled with laughter.
I knew right then
I would want to marry you
every day of my life.

For forty seven years,
I have wished for your tender wrist,
and bosom. For forty seven
lifetimes I have danced near your hip,
and each time I knew you
were meant to fit
into the holes
left by life's detritus.

Come and be near me,
tell me the story of your first word:

Hallelujah.

Sarah **Sandman** is a writing teacher at Indiana University Purdue University Fort Wayne where she teaches all kinds of creative writing. Her favorite class to teach is poetry, and she loves talking about Allen Ginsberg's *Howl*. When she's not reading student work, she writes poetry and creative nonfiction. She also enjoys hiking and drinking too much coffee. She's often seen with children near her, and she will never turn away the chance to pet a dog. Sarah's chapbook, *I Speak Moan*, was published by Finishing Line Press. Right now, she's working on a book length collection of essays. She is also the editor of The Dandelion Review. She lives in Fort Wayne with the love of her life.